HEROIN

AND OTHER POEMS

ALSO BY CHARLIE SMITH

POETRY

Before and After (1995)
The Palms (1993)
Indistinguishable from the Darkness (1990)
Red Roads (1987)

FICTION

Cheap Ticket to Heaven (1996)
Chimney Rock (1993)
Crystal River (1991)
The Lives of the Dead (1990)
Shine Hawk (1988)
Canaan (1985)

HEROIN

AND OTHER POEMS

CHARLIE SMITH

W. W. NORTON & COMPANY

NEW YORK / LONDON

For information about permission to reproduce selections from this book, write to Permissions,
W. W. Norton & Company, Inc., 500 Fifth Avenue, New York, NY 10110

The text of this book is composed in Electra with the display set in Futura
Composition by Gina Webster
Manufacturing by Courier Companies, Inc.
Book design by JAM Design

Library of Congress Cataloging-in-Publication Data

Smith Charlie, 1947–
Heroin and other poems / by Charlie Smith.
p.   cm.
ISBN 0-393-04997-3
I. Title.
PS3569.M5163 H4 2000
811'.54—dc21   00-031871

W. W. Norton & Company, Inc., 500 Fifth Avenue, New York, N.Y. 10110
www.wwnorton.com

W. W. Norton & Company, Ltd., 10 Coptic Street, London WC1A 1PU

1 2 3 4 5 6 7 8 9 0

For dear S.C.—

who got lost

and then found

CONTENTS

ACKNOWLEDGMENTS

Fence: "Of This I Speak to No One"
Five Points: "As for Trees," "Bontemps," "The Submerged Fields"
The Gettysburg Review: "History"
Kenyon Review: "Heroin," "Kicking," "The World as Will and Representation"
The New Republic: "Real Time"
The New Yorker: "Straight," "Yellow Poppies"
The New York Times: "Summertime"
Open City: "Agents of the Moving Company"
The Paris Review: "Los Dos Rancheros"
Poetry: "Beds," "Half-Done World," "Mute," "Planting Morning Glories in
    October," "Poems without Words," "Visitation," "Washington Square"
The Southern Review: "A Near Relation," "Family Burial"
Texas Monthly: "Originations"
The Threepenny Review: "Louisiana Purchase"
Tin House: "Late Return to Miami"
TriQuarterly: "Beautyworks," "Flowers of Manhattan," "Honesty," "Santa Monica"
Western Humanities Review: "At This Hour"
Witness: "I Try to Remember I Am Dying"

"Beds" was reprinted in *Best American Poetry 1997*
"Santa Monica" was reprinted in *The KGB Bar Book of Poems*

To Daniela Serowinski, Michael Block, Maria Carvainis, Jack Levavi,
James McLaughlin, David Williams, Lee Phillips, Nancé Agresta, Annette Cyr,
Moses Hoskins, and friends on Eighty-second and Lafayette Streets—endless thanks.

HEROIN

AND OTHER POEMS

HEROIN

I left a message for my editor to send copies of the contracts
to my new agent,
and then I read a passage about how no one talks
about heroin anymore, and the old life came back to me,
it was early yet, I hadn't used heroin for years,
I was one of the few rural junkies in the nation,
one of the few who tended cattle, there I was
nodding on a rock as the cows, stiff with unendurable shyness,
stumbled up to me. My wife and I would eat mashed potatoes
from the pot and lie out on the porch smoking reefer
until it got too dark to see. I bought the drugs
from my friend at the railroad repair depot
just off the main line from Norfolk, Indochinese material,
Long Bin—to Guam—to Fort Ord—to VA—then by Mr. Fixit train to me,
traveling in a nylon medic's bag. I never trusted
the supply—like love—it could dwindle,
or simply give way,
the flexed utensil, like one of those measuring sticks
you unfold and lay across a map; anybody could step on it.
I loved the graciousness of heroin, the way everything externalized
and obvious in the daylight opened its shirt and revealed its soft pale breasts.
The world slept curled in its own foolhardiness.
And my wife came carefully over the blankets to me and seemed
not to mind who I was. We inserted words
into spaces in the rain. For years I remembered the words
and whispered them to myself, half thinking I might
conjure her back into the world. They never caught us.
We missed them on the way to Mexico, to Puebla,
where eventually the line gave out. We slept on a bench outside a church.
It was two days before she died without regaining consciousness,
as I say in the memoir they are paying me so handsomely for.

REAL TIME

. . . where Hiroshima was, someone said, there's a little star,
and I saw this star, like spit on the sidewalk
. . . and there's a quiet inlet of oaks,
someone said, a brazen light,
and a perpetual return, another promised,
and someone was always having a bad time of it,
grim forecasts and the heart worn down,
punched-in shops on the highway where we bought beer,
and that spring we argued all night,
night after night, and couldn't save the marriage—all that
someone said, will be replaced,
like a city replaced by a meadow
and replaced by a city again—and the little shudder
I got thinking of absent time,
or time without us in it,
and how, sometimes, a friend said, any thought of another
is godlike, is grace, and I read somewhere
about how tired explorers get just before they reach the goal,
about various seaweeds, movies shown in the open air,
about a river pressing in among the trees, and someone said
we all wish to publish manifestos,
and in the decline of summer that year
translations of old ideas appeared like new,
and someone nearly hysterical claimed
he never heard the announcement, and couldn't get out of the way.

LOUISIANA PURCHASE

Who knows but that Meriwether Lewis's
lost diaries might turn up yet
packed in a can in some cramped ex-midden
dug up a thousand years from now,
that elegant, exfoliate style
continue on up the Missouri, into sadness
and disrepute, the suicide in a hotel in Tennessee
no more important now than the bundle
of grasses my friend made out in the woods
yesterday and gave to me after a meeting
in which she confessed she's afraid of everything
that's coming. The past I don't mind, she said,
and laughed as if that was something.

. . . *dissatisfied egotistical state*: Schopenhauer's way of putting things,
thinking about us:
>we are terribly agitated, he says,
no hope for us in good works, or in facts,
>no treehouses or illuminated backyard fetes, no
>>investigations carried on under duress
or played-out hunches described in late-night diners
four hours outside Las Vegas,
will do the trick.

Unable to free ourselves from guilt (we're born guilty)
>our only chance an extreme form of asceticism (quietism, button-upism),
lay low in other words, shake off will and desire, no demands.
>Yet, without the framing of a larger hope, a structure
>that sustains and relieves the pressure of humanness, I wonder
how this is possible.

>S okays art (the experience of art
constitutes cessation of the will:
>>beauty wipes the slate clean),
but what about sports or galloping a horse through a field of lupine,
or reading your long dead unmarried aunt's mail
>>and speculating about "Roberto,"
wondering why she described the days as "voluminous and without delight,"

or the first time you bought reefer,
>or taking the limousine back from a Yankees game,
stopping off for steaks at Frank's on Little West 12th
and seeing some gorgeous woman
get out of a cab and realizing this is your wife?

what of love?

what of tempestuousness and what of tumult,
what of the irresolution of nights on backporches as love spirals down
all around you,

      the bare times of scorn and vituperation,

the losses, the brief asides in which we fill our minds with the glorious mischances
and duplications of someone else's life, where would
           we be (unquiet, fractious) without
these maddening disagreements, men putting things badly,
women addressing the wrong party, junkyards of rust
and dereliction reminding us of our fallibility, the fallibility itself
and the remorse that push us to do better next time,

and what of desire
almost endless,

      and appetite and loss of control

what of
wayward indiscreet possessiveness under big trees in Miami,
or some such place,
her fingers smelling of Cuban spices,
and the way
she turned to say
      she couldn't go on without a kiss?

The idea, he says, is to remove us from time.

Life, according to S, is suffering
and death is its promised land.

What's left is the inner life, salients
and extended peregrinations and long afternoons muttering of conspiracies,
random phrases circulating among the back precincts of thought,
confused ramblings passing as speculation,
                    and speculation itself, the grand moment when
some obscure principle too difficult to repeat or revise begins to make sense, sure,
philosophical systems ground into powder and blown into the eyes of children,

reveries in which we come to understand that true idealism,
                    as S says, "is not the empirical,
                                        but the transcendental."

        "The world is my representation," he says.

I want to be comforted.

I want to leave the house without worrying about what I left
or left unfinished there.

                    Nature, S points out,
accepts us back to its bosom, dead,
without comment.

He means death's not the big deal, we're coming home.

What I mean is I want something to be so true I forget it
and go on fully absorbed out on the dock where the ocean lifts and
falls back sighing.

I notice the gold
streaks on a woman's arm,
the boys boxing under the pines.

STRAIGHT

In all these old photographs sun
shines directly into every face;
it's a rule and makes the past seem
brightly lit, a world exposed and
direct, shadows only in the back,
behind things; and each of them,
men and women once young who are
dead now, children risen from curls
into heavy labor and troubled sleep,
accept this effortlessly; their bodies
look like shields, their faces shine,
and their eyes, looking straight at you,
hold sunlight off like an army; even
pale loitering boys and girls without
charm, women already oppressed beyond
endurance, the big father sprouting
hair on his arms like brushed wire,
in frank sunlight they do not shrink
from, appear touched by a familiar
eternity they don't dream will fail.

LOS DOS RANCHEROS

I can see the moon like a bullet sunk in the clouds' body
and it seems to me the worst has happened. *Nothing*
really touches me, she says and begins to express her contempt.
For a second everything gets transparent. At my cafe breakfast
I sweat profusely and attempt to comfort
the silverware and consider the water, shimmering
in its glass like precious liquid crystal, to be my friend.
When the government cars go by, the big black-curtained cars
containing dignitaries who will one day beg God to save them,
I get up from my seat and stand on the steps looking at the sky
trying not to think of how what was between us—whatever
you call this corybantic—turned up dead this morning,
but it's no use. Now everything refers to it,
including the young man in the Los Dos Rancheros Restaurant
dreaming Puebla or Ixatlan back into shape, who
jabs one song after another into the juke box
hard like a man jabbing his finger into the face
of someone impossible to convince, who halfway to his table
stops to throw his head back and laugh with a sound
like a grease fire smothering. I walk out into the
charmlessly evincerating street
where everyone is doing the best he can to keep the dark
from climbing over his back. *Take your hands off me*,
a woman screams and throws herself out of a car.
Even in sleep, the blind newsdealer says, *my life is confusion.*
From here I plot a course that will take me into an area
in which I am respected and praised for leaving her.
You can look me up, she's saying into the phone when I return,
I am the one who fell in love with the captain and lost her honor

not to mention her fortune and now I live
this retired life, that is to say this life of routine
and memory in which I am without hope. Says this
and gives me a look. Quietly the strangulations begin again.
What do you think? That nothing can kill the world, not even love?

FLOWERS OF MANHATTAN

. . . early morning petal-strewn sidewalks of Manhattan,
honey locust, buckeye, hickory flowers, exotic blooms
from the Korean groceries blown onto sidewalks,
small pale purple scoops and pink delicate purses,
shreds, loops, curled ribbons of magnolia, spikes
and bells, scrawls, clusters of slightly hairy tiny yellow globes . . .
early morning advocacy of life . . . the left side of a walnut tree
glimpsed between ugly ocher buildings, starry petals
of blackberry flowers and the brushy swabs of horse chestnut.
Beyond a clump of Chinese privet with its white flowers
sporting antennaelike sepals topped with gold tabs,
a bush with papery slightly rumpled leaves, an import
never mentioned by comedians or other show business types,
a slender black man takes off his shirt. His skin is smooth
and unmarked and has a deep dusty shine to it. He strokes his chest,
places his hands flat on his breasts and smiles to himself.
He stands under an empress tree just now shedding its
bell-shaped unequally lobed pale purple flowers
that are slightly fragrant, slightly spicy, soft
to the touch (*a handsome, rapidly growing colonial*)
speaking softly. I am overcome suddenly with a desire to
throw my body into the mass of hawthorn flowers
piled up in a bush beside the crooked stone wall. Elders
and black haws, frothy white, are in bloom.
The stately candelabra of the buckeye appear white,
but close up have a yellow cast and are spiked with gold
flanges and smeared with a slightly russet dye. Just now
a woman in wide blue shorts went by screaming. She
carried a sprig of tasseling pine, or this is simply
what I say she carried. I look away from life
for one second and it spurts ahead so suddenly I am bereft
a child abandoned on the trail. There's a whole tree

I don't know the name of shaggy and set upon by white blossoms
like a huge blanket or toupee draping the crest and crown
sliding down the wind-pliant sides, fluttering slightly along the edges
incidentally. Across the island now tuberoses and petunias
have established their first flowerings. Wind stirs
the surface of ponds in Central Park, catches slightly
in various pools dammed against curbs and in low spots
near Sixth and Bleecker. A flare of leftover wild azalea,
the last to be seen this year in Manhattan,
deep in woods beyond the Ramble, flickers and goes out.
Ecstatic thoughts, simple phrases spoken casually but
veering abruptly toward insanity, hearts broken in two,
the mind pushed beyond what it can take, continue as usual.
Spring pounds on the doors. A boy sweeping the sidewalk stops,
makes a fist and throws punches at the air. Love's no secret now.

HONESTY

Maybe Anna won't arrive.
Maybe mordant self-concern will become love.
O you who know things
never change. I imagine
E. A. Poe kissing his child bride, thirteen-year-old girl
her mother standing in for his mother
sweet tempered raking roast potatoes from the fire,
and shiver with tension and morbidity.
He was appalled by loneliness
by scary apartness, shuddering with resentment
and an alarming sense of smothering.
He lived awhile in a bee glade,
high on the island, in NYC.
Anna is
Anna Karenina. Maybe
she won't reach the station.
I used to think the fact my
crazy mother was still alive
meant there was hope. A fool's notion.
She became unreachable
long ago.
In the untidy southern village I come from
this is not unusual.
People are set.
Vietnam was so great, my friend says,
because folks who would never
get a chance to change their minds, did.
Like my friend's father fat ex–Air Force sergeant
who at last, weeping at the grave,
cried Please God end this, it's no good.
Not the *end this* important, but the *it's no good*.

A change of heart.
Not Vronsky saying okay
I didn't mean it, forget the war,
I love you let's get married raise a family,
but Anna.
It's no good. And Edgar Poe,
this weeping into my hat, tugging the sleeve
of a dead child woman: It's no good.

Once in my junkie days I kept a cattle herd.
It was winter in the mountains,
prohibitive, rage like a canvas shirt caked in ice,
I pushed hay bales out of a truck.
The cows, fretful women,
their bony hips, moaning, snotty,
when they snuffled up
I'd punch them in the face.
I wanted to punch
my wife
and the side of the mountain
and my life snarled like a deer in a fence.
I was filled with longing
for joyful permanent fixations, and insight,
for play and a secular individualism,
a spiritual life and some unnameable
opportunity like a right I vaguely
remembered and couldn't get purchase on.
It was no good.
It took me years and one mistake
after another to realize this
and even then I simply got washed out,

put aside
I didn't really learn a lesson.
I know it's not so much the mistakes
not the divisions, or cultural impediments,
the threats and isolation techniques
we run on each other
it's the heart.
My father went to his grave unchanged.
So did Poe.
And beautiful Anna Karenina.
And Ovid. Consuela Concepcion, too, my piano teacher.
They say in the end
Mussolini was so terrified his mind seized and he couldn't speak.
He sat there swelled-up and bug-eyed. This is not it.
Or anyone drowning or
lurching from the fire shrieking he didn't want this to happen.
There is so much gibberish. And imprecision.
No wonder we lock in.
Like you, I get scared.
I used to go to my friend's house,
sink into the old sofa on his back porch
and read all day. His family
and the ducks and dogs would pass by,
let me be—discreet love—I'd feel safe.
It was just after I stumbled out of my second marriage.
My friend practiced a religion
remarkable in its narrow-mindedness. He inserted
his children into this olla podrida
like a man stuffing leaves into a shoe.
It hurt to see it.
Broken saddle bronc of a beautiful face he had
and his wife a slim twist of blonde girl cunning

and fretful without shame
about anything—I spoke up eventually and got tossed.

I've spent years watching television.
I lie on the couch
eating chocolate and watching television,
arguing with some woman in my head.
Television says the world is not a mysterious place.
Don't worry, it says,
you don't have to change a thing.
And then I remember digging wild leeks,
buying eggs from a crippled old lady
who glanced into the next room sadly
as if a great novelist was dying in there,
and went on
talking, like Kissinger after the war.
And how scary things became when my wife
got up close. Change of heart.
Love leeching the lining away, exposing the pulp.
Stupidity and malice
and a fitful generosity,
shortsightedness and painful posturing,
and things continue just as they are,
nut cases, disputes,
overbearing stupid
claims, modernity hamming it up,
life someone says only a device for entering other realms
—all these in the hopper.
And the tough decisions.
Poe dreaming of a cold finger
picking the lock. Anna stuffing screams back down.
Let go, or stay with it?

The Dali Lama saying *Sure, sure, I'll take the sprouts,*
including the Chinese in everything.
My girlfriend stunned by the power of her own rage,
nothing she can do about it yet,
rebuking paradise, groping for the cat.

BEAUTYWORKS

. . . all kinds of beauty in the world dense pressed-down spots in grass,
crabapples scattered on a white sidewalk let me name them,
shadows draped across yellowing lawns, my wife
standing in a barrel to be photographed pretending to scream
is beautiful, my friend who paints with a table knife
endless solid scenes of light, light on the other side of red warehouses,
light in trees preparing the solution to life, light and misrepresentations of light,
and light behind the garage sale and stumbling down a ditch at dawn
such is beauty, and includes dependable father-and-son collection agencies
and my mother who went crazy trying to clean
everything, and a noncom's sudden refusal, copra plantations
and old bomb holes grown up in snakes and yellow flowers,
a lobbyist weeping over his father's cancer,
disputes that never get settled but go on for generations
as a kind of ethnic memory—Moslems never forgiving Christians
for Jerusalem 1099—beauty's like this,
a lingerer at parties, last to get the taste of love out of its mouth,
a friend locked up for his own good, another
sketching naked men, wrestling with his conscience, consortiums
dispersing into colorful anecdotes, frailty of all kinds as if beauty
were erasable, walks on the beach
pondering the uselessness of existence, the endless variety of the natural world
always on the other side of consciousness, no way . . . this is beauty . . .
to understand a thing about it—

SUMMERTIME

I

The sun like a ripped white shirt
drapes the compliant trees; Charlie Parker

on the radio dismantles certain soft pleadings,
and downstairs a woman in her nightgown

is talking quietly of Kansas, of her mother's hands
smeared with butter. It is soft at the edges,

this summer day, indivisible nonetheless,
love's tirade spinning into space.

II

Beyond the city
waves slap and jostle,

a fragrance of sweet cinnamon
moves in from the sea; a young man

dreaming of a fortune turns in sleep
fitfully, presses a wet hand through the side of a car.

It is vague near the sad declarations lovers make,
and the tools of an appropriate

diversion fail to persuade. A scurry
of useless proposals

passes in the shape of messengers bearing gold tureens;
derelict students

caper and preen, longing for night.
The streets shine after rain.

III

Above the West Side the sun
goes brassy and hard, distances magnify.

Children beg at their mother's knees;
it is a time of restraint. Those who draw sustenance

from the reflection of beauty, pull the shades,
like men who have returned from prison,

and weep into their hats. Night comes home
like a boulevardier, and the one you promised to love

is booking her passage to Spain. Rain in the mountains,
someone says, while here, summer,

like a theatrical agent drunk on a spree,
calls everyone it knows. The loveliest face appears,

stamped on a cookie. Poppies litter the walks.
The fat smell of the shops. Light from distant windows

sparkles like gunfire; love
cries from the ditch. A man says

IV

Everything is holy
and tries to mean what he says.

BEDS

Terrible beds, soft beds, wily, elusive beds,
beds of half-grown boys, fey and trembling,
    dumped on their ear beds of traveling salesmen surprised,
girl beds and virginal young woman beds,
    matronal expansively expressed beds, I think of these,
recalled to sleep, out of sleep into sleep,
    waked early, waked late at night remembering,
drunken beds, sopping watery beds, pissed-in beds,
    beds come to me, all I have slept in,
beds I have knelt beside and dreamed of,
    bench one foot wide for a bed in Saipan,
hay barn in Turkey bed, dawn like sherbet
    naked men stood up out of, trickling weedy beds,
greetings and good-byes from beds,
    sullen, imperious beds . . . there was always a bed,
place to lie down, if only for a pause, in jail
    or in the aisle of a bus, berths below decks
diesel smoke and topside typhoon,
    Pacific swells, trough and deep six beds for lost sailors,
mountain beds often cold and wet,
    sooty nights risen from bed drunk
whirling in the yard lie abed in grass
    or among tomato vines and springy corn
love gone from my bed
    love lost to another's, searching the cold
fabrications for clues, bed stains
    and scented sheets, beds of humiliation
and scorn, shivering clothed in unheat until dawn
    friend appearing through white cloud said
Go now to the neighbors . . . hot bath like a bed,
    and beds of fern and moss
and pine boughs, beds in Istanbul Hotel plush

and beds in Florence and golden Madrid,
southern beds and beds in New England tucked under quilts,
    cornfed beds and *lit de cassis,* and narrow bed of devotion,
bed of love, of endurance,
    bed of turmoil and surrender
and change slow to come,
    bed of low spoken phrases,
bed of form become style
    bed of California grape arbors
and outdoor beds and beds on porches
    and beds in back bedrooms where the crazy son died
beds in attics and in upper stories down long stone corridors
    beds that trembled and bunk beds
and beds without meaning
    beds in trees,
in grass, in fields of clover
    beds in fragrant lover's arms,
beds multiplied into
    nights sleepless and disordered in beds,
into nights of confusion and dismay,
    of lust
of hatred and pride mixed in a sour beam
    of persistence, nights of fear,
nights of memory
    and applicable recall,
nights of kisses, nights of frankness
    passing for truth, nights of delightful smells,
nights on the river, by the sea, inland nights
    spoken of in hushed voices, nights by the wayside,
nights come to bed late for no reason,
    nights spent for a time sitting on the bathroom floor,

nights and days and the next night in bed
  recovering from serious illness, in beds without exits,
beds stepped bold up to, beds
  unfolding like mysteries, childhood beds,
the beds of adulthood and youth,
  Chinese beds, decent Norwegian beds,
Filipino tropical beds,
  stained beds, beds soaked in perfume, striped
and checkered beds, all night spent
  beside someone's bed, beside beds of loved ones,
the bed my father died in burned the next day
  in a pit behind the house, my mother's bed empty
for years, beds of my wives, beds of children
  raised from their beds and sent forth into the world,
soft and ample and undivided beds,
  nights lingering quietly in the mind,
beds you spoke of as we lay after supper calm in our bed
  listening to night come down around us,
settled and consonant, happy in our bed.

FISTFIGHT

Thinking of what it's like to wake alone at the end of your life
as my mother and so many others do,
old men
coming to on stoops and under arcades indiscriminately
in whitened New York dawns,
old women lying awake in narrow beds
on psych wards
listening to memory sing its thin menacing songs

thinking too of morning on riverbanks
waking in the poised irrepressible superannuated light,
of the tug
of current on my ankles as I wade out to dip water for coffee,
thinking of the story I wrote about this,
of a woman
in this story who was unrecoverable
and of how other women
disliked me for writing about her as I did,
and how
when someone told me this I sat there quietly,
slightly mortified
and unsure how to respond (now it's all right)

thinking of those years I sat around waiting for something to happen,
and the years in the South we all tried to escape from
and couldn't

drifting on from this
to car trips

to arguments first thing in the morning
when you stand naked before your naked lover shrieking,

to old men in World War II uniforms
tottering before mirrors among boxes and bales of golf magazines
giving orders to ghosts

to my mother
running hot water over her hands

returning in this period of helplessness and devotion
to my (ex-) lover
alone in her kitchen eating soup,
tapping the spoon against her lip,
saying the name
of her brother (the one who went crazy) inaudibly to herself.

FAMILY BURIAL

All around water moves, rocking . . .
        slide of river, current a snake descending the tree,
               meets the tide returning after a night in the
               wilderness . . .
men reveal themselves only with great reluctance,
take years to tell a friend,
change of heart that for some comes snapped upright
and smoldering for others appears gradually
over years so slowly nothing's different, we recall
another arrangement perhaps, candles the color of sunshine,
a small basket of silver rings, tall columns of amber light
        love slipped through . . .
               not until Father died, the river says, did I know I
               could live.

MUTE

It's gotten so I can't say what's in my heart
and substitute high-flown brooding
and complex notions concerning the rhythm behind certain actions.
I take walks a couple of times a day,
in early afternoon and later
just before dark and try to pay attention to selected vegetation
and chairs on porches, abandoned board games, and to the attitudes
about life expressed in the postures of husbands and wives
passing, to whatever
else is moving about, to dogs, to the cats this town is filled with.
I am unable to bring myself to speak to anyone,
or perhaps I speak abruptly to a clerk in a store where I buy a cup of coffee
and walk away afraid I have been harsh with him,
which is the greatest sin,
yet I would like to stop someone and say
I have been in love like you
or I think there is a divine expression coming through
all things, no matter how ridiculous they seem,
but I am unable to do this, I simply keep walking.
It may be just after noon when only old men sit outside
because they can't
stand being alone indoors another minute
or it may be dusk when the darkness is like wings being folded
in the gumbo-limbo trees
and whoever I pass is almost unrecognizable to me
as I am to them. I say nothing
and hinder no one. You can hear doves
repeating their stupid cries in the pines.

CALLING FOR CLARE

I survey my manuscripts for flaws in judgment,
for some hint of what I might really mean,
and then, unsatisfied by this,
I lie in the dark, the semidark,
listening to the airwaves,
listening for something familiar,
some exclusive.
I know my hands smell of reproach
and humiliation,
and it is no leap to admit
I have begun to apologize to buildings and whole districts,
to trees and to the people standing under them,
but still I am afraid I have missed something crucial,
some valid point,
in my dead brother's phrase,
that entered the discussion a while back
and changed everything.
I have cultivated an approach
obviously out of step with my peers, but I can't stop now.
I mean I have stopped now.
We could go into my room if you like
and discuss absence.
A number of important concepts and entities
are missing.
We might press an ear to the wall
and listen to next door's desperate case. He's sobbing again
and calling for Clare.
Afterwards we can taunt ourselves
with near misses.
Recently someone—I swear it's not me—
was seen crawling along a darkened corridor.
I myself was fired,

so I'm told, from various jobs
I never applied for, or held.
Someone else is picking up
my check. And D's in my thoughts again,
somehow she's
found her way back there.
My thoughts of Maine
and its coarse conifery and moose habitat,
its unsolved mysteries and streets emptied by rain.

AS FOR TREES

. . . there are the stupendous oaks and hickories I climbed,
catafalques and monuments, broken-down harassed improvident trees,
unconnected, poorly constructed unsought-after trees, there are bundled sticks,

shaken willows, river birches without footings and over-investigated,
dramatized firs, celibate, virginal pines, capacious elms,
birches divided against themselves, groves come up short, repudiated locusts,

there are maples and obvious sycamores, poplars slender as tax collectors,
duplicated laurels, chinaberry, redwoods without scruples, divisive, whining persimmons,
trees of legend and saplings writhing as if on fire,

                                        there are saucy, duplicitous conifers,

everyday live oaks, trees with limbs like thighs, like torsos, like dolphins
rotting on a dock, trees made of deerhide and pleurisy, trees without meaning
beyond the noise they make, there are sumac and buckeye and hawthorn of the rose family,

there's mulberry my girlfriend eats of, there is a tree
with no name, there are druidical subversive trees, trees the old man
thinks of when he walks around at night whistling,

                                        there is Sherwood Forest and

delayed reactions taking place under trees,

                                        there is a large following

 for some trees, flower and fruit, there are roots poking from the ground,
there is the holly & the effervescent plum, bamboo, lignum vitae, crabapple, chokecherry & bay,

there are the trees I have slept under, trees lightning loves, luxurious undulant trees,
immaculate trees and dogwoods forlorn and white-headed in the spring woods,
there are trees in various locales unthought of, trees at the dump and camphor trees

in graveyards & companionable junipers & redbuds & Japanese magnolias and crepe myrtle &
dahoon, tupelo, viburnum, spruce, catalpa and gum,

                                        there are loquacious trees

and trees that fidget and trees that seem to move around at night,
and voices coming from trees and the famous Cedars of Lebanon,

and there are the inveterate hustlers, the trees with red berries and there are
trees like Italian laughter, and unbedded trees, and pepper trees and trees by the ocean
and beeches behind the dunes,

                    there's rhododendron and laurel, basswood and hop hornbeam

there's yucca and coral tree,

                        eternal trees and golden trees and trees sewn up tight
and undetectable trees and cautious, dependable trees, and there are fruits
fallen close to the tree and accidents of birth, and trees like hogs run through,

and there is the tree I kissed my first wife under
and the tree she remembered and her red-stained mouth,

there is my friend buried under a myrtle tree, and there's the sand hickory
and the pecan and the raccoon in the loblolly pine, and there are the laurel, black haw, cherry
    and mountain ash and the box elder torn down by hurricane,

there're more trees in the Smokies than anywhere else, there are
trees colossal in their own minds,
sacrificed trees, stumps and root systems upended on ranches,

there is hemlock and silver bell and sparkleberry and peach,
mimosas come to mind, and the obvious silk tree, I saw a tamarack once,
and at the botanical gardens there are banyan trees and baobabs and a cypress

                                                                like the cypress
on Christopher Street,

there are locust pods like arched black eyebrows of amazed seigneurs,
and there are the brittle limbs of the London plane tree,

there are simple quivering trees and foxhaven trees and there's a tree
in the middle of my second wife's living room,

there is sassafras, yaupon and pear, there are trees we all love,
cottonwoods and the fragile chestnut, doomed to die, trees that linger
like Spanish perfume,

                         and there are trees getting things together finally
and trees marshaling their forces and there are trees without hope,
losers and touts down on their luck

                              and there's an ailanthus behind the
Jesu Christo Es El Senor Liquor Store, a spindly tree, smoke-bit and softened up
by winter, a tree we could go without noticing, and in sooty backyards

there are flowering fruit trees and there's buckthorn and fig, codicils
and allusions to trees and the brief aside once about a tree in the mind,
African and European trees, walnut trees and butternut, hapless trees once human,

there's a rumor about trees and someone mutters like a tree muttering to the wind,

there are corolla, calyx and sepals, red-bit or yellow, white as a sheet falling,

we distinguish various shapes for leaves, the round and the spearlike lance, the
egg-shaped and the frog-footed, the simple leaves of chokecherry and sourwood droop in
summer, juniper leaves threadlike or stiff & bony, needles blunted,
                                                                    hugging the ground in winter,

there are leaves euphonious, sighing leaves, whistling, soughing, moaning leaves,
whole boughs moving as if about to exit the earth, rattling of palms,
clatter of magnolias, radiant buckeye leaves as if offering five paths,

there are the meaningless confidential remarks, the questing of pines, forthright pistachios,
the obstinate oaks, the complicated stirring of the honey locust,
there are catkins and bouquets, single florets dipped in wax,

spatters of scarlet in the white, vague yellow musings, blue silk bits,
rouged lip skin peeled off and crumpled up,
                                        there are

calcified leaves and flowers without distinction and strings of yellow
in late spring, and bunches and unstrung wreaths, stalks of red and yellow,
creamy blisterings, there are petals in her hair,

there are acorns and multitudes of purple berries and illiterate pignuts and prickly filberts,
buckeyes and tufted sycamore balls, various pods, peas of all sizes, tough horned pellets
and sheathes discarded, husks and hulls, burst maple cases

                                        and the shredded dresses of virginal alders,
carelessly tossed aside, coats and leggings, shoes, slippers, scabbards, and smashed violins,
there are the round red berries of the possum haw,

and the splashy, lyric fruits,
I could mention these, epic groves,
fall rattling up its ladders to set fire in the trees.

OF THIS I SPEAK TO NO ONE

Some days the rage
like a fire in the back of the house,
burning up the baby clothes after you're so spent
and ragged out with misery you set a fire in the pump room,
pour kerosene over the little playsuits
and blue bunny pants your mother sent
and stand there stoned & crying, saying *impossible impossible.*
I have been screaming all day in my head
and then I hit the dog across the back
attempting to train it to love me,
the dog that is now scared of me and can't stay
away from the garbage, who lives at the neighbors'
and stands on their front porch looking impassively at me,
like a friend who believes the baseless charges.
Of this I can speak to no one, as you
can't speak of the crows and the terrible thoughts
coming out of the woods like old men in gray suits.
Each night we are exchanged
for something much worse than we imagined,
which is why late in the day
I go out to the woods where the poplars are greasy
and the oaks are against me
and lie down across the grain of the mountain cursing,
trying to tear the itch off my hands.
The day's gigantic misunderstanding of everything I have said
goes on relentlessly.
Of the smells that are killing me
and the favors my head keeps asking,
the attempts at reconciliation the dark keeps proposing,
the terrifying questions,
and the way the road to town simply hangs in the air,
of the rain getting colder in a season

without issue,
and Berlioz inconsolable on the radio,
of the negotiations going badly,
and an old man squatting in a field
nicking the boll of an opium flower, licking his thumb—
the mortification—of these I say nothing.

Blue mountainous clouds
at the end of the street, a coppery
sheen below that,
below that straight brown lines, gray,
a shifting white bit in the corner
where the bay
slaps itself. Late sun drains
one side of Manhattan, slips off
to distant parts
as revelers and late risers walk off
their divisions, come together
with themselves.
Tourists jostle
like fitful birds settling for the
night.
Brooklyn waterfront, Governors Island
are crusted with mechanical devices,
docks,
and cranes with their arms folded back.
Dusk brings its colorful peace to
the lower
parts of the island, settles small
disputes of daylight
around the fish market, leans hard
against certain buildings
and retires. There's a tremendous
sense of opportunity,
a hope for connection and power,
but this too
is only passing. An old friend's
apartment's for rent, there's a sign;
he's in another wing, upset by his

failure
to rise; his wife supports the family
and hates it.
Small stories get told
by the waterworks. Some try on
sweaters
from barrows and look at themselves
in plate glass.
Girls give testy smiles. Another's
wild look sticks in the mind.
Later, as neon translates the early
works of the dark,
a man remembers a clue to life,
can't state it and stands baffled
six feet
from a woman who just lost a child
to disease.
The fish special is getting older
as we speak.
"Time embodies nothing," a small man
says, passing
a look to the woman in the third chair
from the right. You can smell
the brine in the air.
Someone's brought a small yellow
dog with him,
a conversation piece momentarily
that everyone ignores
except for a young woman wearing spats;
she takes
up the dog and begins a story

of loss she heard as a child; it
        gets late.
A shift in perspective brings the stars
        out, a few.
Agitation passes for expectancy. Someone
        senses
a heart attack coming on and begins
        to pray.
A glow in the east is only the lights
        of a nightclub.
Pressure subsides, begins to rebuild,
        arguments
flare in tiny cafes. Someone loses
        his temper
and says what should never be
        said. The key to her heart
lies unclaimed by a fence under the
        Brooklyn Bridge.
A young man finds it there.

THE TRAIL

In cities you never visited I sensed your presence.
In bungalow colonies and airport delicatessens

I caught sight of someone
who might have been you, but I couldn't catch up.

I rented apartments and left them vacant in hopes
you might appear, like a vision.

In Utah, a ridgeline seemed to be leading toward you,
but I was wrong.

I tried each highway, driving slowly
so as not to miss you if you'd pulled over to rest.

I descended into coastal cities, often at dawn,
and sat in coffee shops waiting for you.

In hotel rooms
I watched for the phone's blinking light.

I tried to be precise, and maintain confidence,
repeating supportive phrases from my reading,

attempting to stay calm, but often I fell to pieces.
I encountered conscripts and justifiers like myself,

apparitions shouting their news into traffic,
but nothing they told me touched on you.

I eavesdropped on conversations, listening
for the choked-down sobs of the grief-stricken.

Up on the mesa, by a motel pool, I read a story outloud,
a tale in which the author wrote eloquently

of the queerly resolute heroine's
quiet life in a cabin by a meadow,

where the fall, still cordial to its summer,
had begun to streak the poplars faintly gold.

Even then—and I tried hard—
I couldn't picture you.

A NEAR RELATION

For months after it happened my brother sent gifts
packed in huge quantities of balled-up paper and plastic pellets,
as if the packing itself was emblem of
the encapsulating and preservationist feelings he bore me,
or as if the boxes contained the priceless history of our past
or the years of brotherhood come down to a fistfight.
He wanted me to root through the shredded local papers,
through the polyethylene sawdust and sliced up Christmas wrappings,
through the advertisements for liniment that had never failed
and back braces and show dogs with the mange now cured,
to discover his indestructible love for me
in the small square boxes of broken pecan meats,
in the collections of local treasures including tiny fish skeletons,
dragonfly wings and a stylized piece of rock shaped like a thumb,
or in the jar of tupelo honey the color of gold mixed with tea
that was, so the circular said, absolutely pure, inviolate, without taint
and wouldn't turn to sugar, stiffen into lumps or disappoint in any way.
I didn't respond. Then in the spring he sent a snapshot of his wife.
In the photo she stood in shallow water
looking straight at the camera. It was one of those pictures
a man saves out for himself after the marriage breaks down,
saves for the time when he is strong enough again
to entertain his loss, to return like a desolated child
to the everlasting perfection of the woman's body, and stare at it.
I know how it takes everything out of you, he says to himself,
to look at her who no longer belongs to you—who belongs to no one you know—
and realize you will never be allowed to speak to her again
in this life, will never be allowed anything with her again in this life,
no matter what changes or how you spruce up your derelict morbid unforgivable self.
I know my brother wants me to study this picture.
He wants me to see the vast unapproachable beauty revealed before me.

The delicacy and strength, the honey-colored imperturbable skin
and the frank invitation in her brown eyes.
A propped canoe paddle angles in under her chin
like a yellow lance penetrating her skull, but she is smiling.

INDIANS DRIVING PICKUP TRUCKS

I have this complicated friend who teaches poetry at H—.
She takes time off regularly and drives nonstop
to New Mexico where she sets up in an old adobe
and furiously writes stories about women thumbing rides
through the desert, women who climb in with Indians
driving pickup trucks, are taken back to the rez for treatment,
love treatment and such, and then spend years out there
with their hair in a twist, raking in the yard.

She loves this material and hates her life, she says.
Each day, she says, *is like a door I plunge out of, on fire.*
You wouldn't believe what goes on under this breastbone.
And hits her chest with a thumb knuckle.

She cleans everything out of the house and
then sits on the floor writing into a blue notebook.
It's an entirely empty house, two rooms—in New Mexico—
up on the mesa, under a strict blue sky.
Outside men in pickup trucks throw beer bottles
at the stop sign. She doesn't look up,
or maybe she looks up,
but everything right now is a piece of mental magic
so what can they do to her?

I remember when she was young,
the morning I picked her up at the jail and she was leaning
over the counter cursing the clerk and
pulling everything out of the envelope they gave her and throwing it
on the floor screaming until somebody had to come out
and put her back in the cell. That was before she sobered up.
Now she's mild in manner, almost meek, though very opinionated.

She loves these women she writes about,
these rough women raking the bare clay
of some meager Indian domicile who with their hard eyes
and stubbornness are making the best of it.
Everything behind, she writes, *was dead and gone,*
and nothing ahead meant anything.
Grass fires in the distance, the road like a white weathered plank,
and over in the sweathouse, Crazyhorse coming to.

I tell myself
about how I won't see Miami
again, or my nephews crunching celery,
I won't talk about Robert Kennedy
or tramp through the marsh
to whales
beached and black on an empty
shore. I pray and
meditate, concentrate on death,
watch certain programs
concerned with failed operations,
point out the way a beauty's face
sags, the stiff
walk of a former lover. I
promote retirement,
attend funerals,
dial my dead mother's number
and harangue the new family
that's got it.
I whisper to a child,
faint with delight,
that I'm a dead man.
He looks at me with contempt,
but I go on talking,
sure I can convince him,
sure I can see, like
a fleck of blood in his eye,
the fatal wound.

BASIC BLACK

For simplicity's sake
I walk out in the backyard, poke among the pecan leaves,
eye the twilit moths above the syringa.
Should I budget my time?
Beg God to send her back? How can I change?
The path—I'm following a path—leads by a bamboo thicket.
A bit of leftover sun
festers in the pinnate tops of the bamboo.
Small brown squall of squirrel's nest in the sweet gum.
The land sinks toward the water. Black water river,
black in daylight, basic black,
no need to dress for the dark.
At night the water blends in. All this in my mind
as I sit in the house thinking. Lotus blossoms are white,
and appear to float.

SCHUBERT IN FLORIDA

        I was listening
to Schubert, I was standing in a stairwell
in a beach town, listening to Schubert's darkest sonata
played on a car radio,
        thinking of children
coming on love for the first time, of their hands
trembling as they reach across an obscure space
to touch the beloved who has become everything
important in life,
        and thought how ridiculous
and destructive this is, this irrepressible need
for the loved one, the cascade through the self
of another's presence —
        thinking of the music
picking a way through this like a man searching
tearfully for his most important possession, a man drifting
through one of the aging Florida beach towns
on an August day
        who abruptly leaves the dolphin performance
and returns to his car
parked in the shade of a gumbo-limbo tree and takes a nap
        & dreams of his ex-wife crossing a sun-streaked lawn,
a fine woman who glances at him without desire
        as one would glance
indifferently at a stranger standing in a outdoor stairwell
in a beach town listening to Schubert played on a car radio,
        a stranger waiting almost patiently for a brief sadness
to quell and die down, so he might move on from there.

VOLUTE

I pull down the internal wallpaper
gut the structure
I want a bare lot, take all the elements
& effects of civilization back I don't need them
return the porch, the footings, return
the garden the duck with the clacking wind-turned wings
return the driveway & the insubstantial fescue
& border shrubs take them back
to prairie, to the low rolling hills of origin,
I suggest you reintegrate this patch with its lost ancestors
its vast former life, a sense of endlessness
of time and space, random motion, bugs hanging
from grass stems, voles and rabbits, thunder of storms
& buffalo no lapidated hearts —

KICKING

When we broke up I removed all traces from the house.
The little plastic vials, the inside out glassine bags
stamped with names: CORVETTE, GRAND PRIX, LEMANS,
dumped the hospital tubing and three blood-stained belts and
the book on medieval farming I used to read
like a lullaby. *I never loved you,*
the furniture said, *I always hated you,*
and all the plants coarsely mocked me.
I waked up with hands hanging from my throat
somewhere applause dying out, the hole getting bigger.
And ground down the space between
us for weeks with women, call them women,
but the minute I was out their door
the hole gaped again, like a pocketbook torn open by a thief. I raged
through the house, explained to the open refrigerator how misused I was,
wept into my hands, puked, sweat the shame
into my sheets, studied my horoscope, scoured texts
in film and print, attended showcases for the chemically deranged,
complied with whatever I was told, got a haircut,
listened to whatever song
said the world was an impossible place, prayed, dreamed—
and was glad, even in the worst dreams,
when I saw the spike—bespoke it
among friends, admitted the stupid maniacal ignorant impossible notions
behind the whole thing,
and was often hurled suddenly a thousand
miles an hour at the desire simply to look at you. Old Horse.
My friend knew a woman getting clean
who stuffed rags into her lover's gas tank
and blew up a block's worth of cars. Another form of undistinguished
pleading, he called it, and laughed. But it's nothing, nothing.

Years ago, just before I left for the war,
a friend and I drove to Jacksonville Beach
and walked out onto the strand
where Hurricane Doreen had whipped the surf
into suds against the breakwater
and the big ocean buoys, as large as tractors, rolled in the waves.
I was bereft then too & men were dying & the wind blew none of it away.

THREE DAYS OUT

I like the straightforward red dahlias best,
not the white ones or the peppermint or the
red-streaked yellow, or the straight yellow.
I like the red, they're best, but I also check
the cornflowers, check statice and marigolds,
daisies, the flowers that look like pieces
of sucked yellow candy; and all the branches
with berries on them, I check them too, touch
the holly and the bittersweet and the oak
branches with red leaves attached. I need
some flowers so I will feel better about things,
it's not so unusual. Tired of the drab, ten
minutes into a new life I'm worn out. My sick
spirit's like a chopped up body—a loved one's
body—I carry around in a suitcase. I want flowers
for this, it gives me something to do, going to
the stands asking questions. How much are those?
What *are* those? Little blue Mexican temple hats
on a leafy stick. Whisks and shreds. You can
see how the plants once thought they were heirs
to the kingdom. Before the animals, before us.
A sovereignty of color and form. Royal personages
torn open by the roadside, the beautiful colors,
the intricate collocation, slashes of red and blue,
the disaster you can't tear your eyes from.

ZEN DO

They are teaching us to stay put, as Mother did
in the oh so long ago when her lips tasted of raspberries.
Gradually the trash fires of metaphysics die out.
Behind each of us, we're told, a bank shelves away.
Beyond this a vastness opens.
Yesterday the woods bled all day.
Conversion of thought into a thin gold wedge
is multiple and serial and endless.
Who advances credit for one whose name is not registered,
whose footprints are his only currency?
I sink into the dew to see what my body will leave behind.
At dawn I go out on the lawn
and shadow box with the green metal Buddha
who does not notice the world crept like a cat into his arms.

HEROIN II

No monster in the knife drawer
or the medicine cabinet or the icy woods,
or in a turn for the worse,
         no back stairs kicked loose
by a madman: nothing here but firelight
explaining itself on your face, and dreams we have
of wild animals come into the house
                     as if they love us
now, gentled by drugs, who sit with us like merciful children;

and the way you stretch your body like something expensive
& carefully considered,
         about to be put away
for the night, and the way the night continues
despite everything we say about it, a majestic presence
in itself: and the arch of your neck like a natural bridge
joining this farm & heaven—worlds unopposable—the stories
we tell trailing off into murmurs
                     & long defenestrating silences
in which great shifts of perspective take place,

and the dog, vacationing next door this week,
and the way we wrote letters
         all one fall
and overcame each one as we wrote it,
and carried them to the mailbox
and hid in the bushes by the road
                     waiting for the substitute mailman,
the one who said the dead fields were beautiful, to find them.

AGENTS OF THE MOVING COMPANY

Rain: morning wadded in a corner,
thickening above the trees'
new versions. Still the same early morning walkers,
dogs trotting along under umbrellas,
servicemen slapping themselves awake
and representatives of the oil company or plumbers in dark blue
uniforms
approaching pipes.
I think about friends who keep diaries,
and those whose lives are impossible, how hard it is to live with dignity,
retain a sense of life as renewing itself,
grace. When I failed
I wanted friends to join me, give up ambition, step back. I drank
for years, finally changed my mind
and started over then years later
failed again. No drinks now but the same envy mixed with shame,
still the same familiar unhappy laughter
I recognize, from
others fallen short; —one friend goes bitterly on about
his lack of success,
drifts to the hors d'ouvres and stands there
waiting for fortune to find him. I continue my calculations,
think of changing my name,
heading off in a slightly different direction.
I sense the querulousness of age, the disappointments
converted into a reactionary philosophy
hard to take
by any but the deranged, the petrific glare
maintained through changes in weather,
love's ministrations (the dumb
staring, the blanks) ineffective.
You can make a list of what's enviable:

form, religion,
family, pension checks like handkerchiefs drying on a mirror,
friends, a sense of fun.
I know a man who knows everything about basketball.
Another dabbles in computers, exchanges E-letters
with women whose dead husbands were nuts.
One day my next-door neighbor
wheeled from her house
went fluttering in nightclothes through the park.
Someone not the city a relative I think came for her,
she's not been heard from since. I know it doesn't matter,
when you break down, if the cabinets and the crockery talk to you
or if you talk back arguing a point of courtesy.
Eventually we hope only for freedom from terror,
that the conversation might die out into a genial (or slightly quizzical)
gaze held steady for a while
then fading like sunlight sinking among the nasturtiums.

PLANTING MORNING GLORIES IN OCTOBER

Black seed-sputter, peppercorns
I shake from the papery shingle and poke into pot earth.
Grace in October, and sunlight, water drops,
bring them up. Empires of morning glory,
farm enchantments bugle tissue flower
w/ five-pointed star, pale blue & royal blue, plush velvet color
among heart-shaped leaves & stringy enwrapped, circumlocuted vines.
Once fence sitters, shucked out of fall's disasters
on the Lower East Side wandering with a friend
& brought home to the highrise
set in pots and conjured quick into light.
Can't wait for spring on this.
Massive in their native setting, they crimp
and skinnify here, flourish. Soon—by the holidays—
I'll gather the whole ruckus up in my arms,
pert blooms foiled by noon light, rolled like silk pennants
each morning unfurled—all forgiven in the night—shining.

ORIGINATIONS

My grandfather, arrested on the Ochlockonee for setting illegal traps,
    last of the river poachers, couldn't be stopped, took nutria, beaver,
otter, set trotlines, netted mullet out of season, slaughtered deer
    for the Tallahassee restaurant trade, killed the last bear in Leon County,
in Waucusa, in Wakulla and Alachua, Walker counties. He fought his brother,
    a sharpie lawyer, churchman, lost again & again.
In the BK Baptist Church bare pine boards weathering to gold, hand hewn
    and hand adzed and sanded cypress benches, heavy as iron, cypress pulpit,
plank floor painted blue, church my parents, my brothers
    were married in, church my grandfather had a fistfight in, broke the right hand
of his best friend with a hammer & got knocked out
    by his best friend's leftover good hand. My grandfather waked up laughing.

One thing originates another, squirrel stew
    and the smell of biscuits on a fall afternoon, an old black man
licking stamps for a letter to his son, off in college
    who will be killed in a bus accident north of Calcutta. In his suitcase
a letter from an Indian poet, a woman
    hysterically berating him for crimes that will go undiscovered.
And the father, an old man when his son was born,
    gets down on his knees in the garden & begins to lick the leaves
of the bean plants, & crawls up under the squash vines & lies there
    for two days. Snakes crawl over him, & the sun burns his neck,
& his son seems alive to him in the dust, like a smell, or a wisp
    floating like caterpillar webs in the pecan trees. One thing leads to another,
he thinks, and remembers the girl who bore the child,
    taking the child from her, her fright and tears, her coming to the house
begging him to give the baby back, & he wouldn't, he was stronger,
    had money, he would raise his own child, and did raise him.
The girl moved away. & now I have what's left, the burned body in a crate,
    ashes and remnants buried outside town behind a church he never attends.

& my grandfather crossing this man's land,
     a corner below the cedar woods, & the old man taking a shot at him,
almost too far away to hit, & my grandfather turning back,
     frightened at last, by a splinter hole in a tree.

When I was a child I'd sit on the front steps waiting for my grandfather.
     We couldn't go into his room.
He'd come out after midday, sit in the shade
     in a big rocker smoking a pipe, gauging distance
and memory with level gray eyes.
     Sometimes he'd talk, but mostly not.
My mother worshipped him, brought him gifts.
     He saw Robert E. Lee once, sitting on a horse,
and recalled how short-legged he was.
     My grandfather like water in a carved cup, still.
& his brother dying in an old house on the river in flood time,
     water rising into the first floor, rising to the level of the bed
and soaking the bed, the brother too sick
     to move, lying in water his head propped on a golden pillow, dreaming.
& my father, on a sunny day in June,
     sitting on the floor beside
his stack of books, the histories he'd written, and shooting himself.
     & Mother falling to her knees in the yard,
never herself again, someone on drugs,
     her father never the same, her mother dead by heart attack,
my brother slapped in the face in a bar outside Kansas City,
     who returned later with a gun and shot two men & was put in prison for twelve years
and never spoke to any of us again. "My wife's from Kansas City,"
     my friend says, "she probably remembers all that."

YELLOW POPPIES

I'm mortally impatient for the past to catch up to me,
for it to go by like a loud car boiling down a dirt road,
a car you hook from a snatch of clattery music, bright glimpse
of a face that looks, maybe it is, beautiful . . .

I remember everything, but I don't want to.

I've tried to say nothing, but sometimes a fact
or what I remember as a fact slips out, a bit about
my mother that makes her seem mean-spirited, selfish,
or another about one of my brothers licking blood off his arm.

I went up to the country, there were artisans,
each with a family, cars in the driveway with bumper stickers
admonishing everyone behind them to straighten up in some way,
and I thought, There's a group I don't want to be part of.

But such thoughts are unkind and don't really help.

My father wasn't a war hero,
but he wished he was. My mother was a beauty,
but more of a party girl than a beauty, the smoky type
who would accompany you to the beach
and later argue with you, her eyes flashing,
until you were sorry you met her.
                              Each instance
today seems connected to some occurrence in the past,
and I think sometimes this is a pattern almost like the figure
of imagination itself, the way imagination is the recognition
of unacknowledged correspondences, things lining up,
in other words, like the memory of this afternoon's shower,
in a few hours already a memory of sun streaking the wet grass,

the grass gold like the backs of the hunting dogs, dogs
you saw once at the edge of the pond, milling around her,
or the way the human voice, her voice, say,
could become like a bird's, the way at night sometimes
you could hear her whistling as she returned from a walk,
and you could tell from the sound, even though it was late
and we were far in the country, she had found
a way to make herself happy, for a time, out in the dark.

MOON, MOON

The moon follows me street by street—
the same moon with its Camembert and blue face,
blue-eyed moon—or a new moon each street,
one per street—whichever it is
I'm faithful to the one I see, singing "Moon River,"
as I go, walking the streets, faithful to the one
I'm with at the moment I'm with her—I'm with
no one now—I take the moon for a symbol of devotion tonight,
of love's grace, moon over the East River,
Hudson delta, over the Atlantic where hurricane's
despoiling an empty patch of sea, warming up—

tonight there's moonlight in the city, pale effusion
upon the shoulders of drummed-out lovers
and torture victims—upon the priest rolling
up a badminton net,
the child teaching herself to pray—
equal opportunity moon, moon of Puerto Rican gangsters
playing dance tunes before work,
moon of the emotionally demolished and crazy—
impeccable moon—vast and uncluttered, moon
of silent blue seas, moon of Asia and its
outlying dependencies—of the Americas & Europe—
chiseled African moon—it's a rock in night's shoe,
light left on in the closet I enter to
root through love's used up materials
and scrawled utterances—my pleas for reconsideration—
(moon my companion of demented nights
at the pay phone dialing her number . . .)—witness
to the fulgarious *pecca vis* of love—
strabismic moon, you might say, same moon

as in the stories, distant self-contained wilderness
or astral dumping ground—can't-make-it-
on-its-own moon—like me, accepting all compliments,
stubborn, yet quick to take offense, abashed
and fretful moon, moon white with anger—with fright—
incidental moon, you might say—what's left,
I think, thinking of the moon
as I head south across the city, of love
squeezed in a fist—
call it love—white chunk
of gravel in the nightbird's crop—
only one per customer (moon), yet always available,
the two of us not afraid to show our faces, moon,
neither checking out yet on the other, or on life
(this mainly what I'm thinking about—life,
checking out on it, as if down streets
slanting into a mine,
going down, dear, to explore my
mineral wealth—ha ha—
one who's had enough of trickery and
love snatched from his hands—fix that, moon—)
still here, bobbing up—white apple, head
of a newborn baby, moon shaped like a city—
shining on millionaires recently stripped of their holdings,
on the last customer in Show World, picking the dried
moon fizz from his fingers—egg, imponderable,
bull's-eye—I'm faithful to you tonight, moon,
one more undependable lover
talking a stroll, pretending to walk it off,
headed into the rural districts,
of Central Park, that is, toward the little
homesteads brightened by longing

and flashlights—cracked, moony hearts
sputtering like engines about to fail—

you'll find me stretched out on the grass, dear,
singing "Moon over Charlie,"
supine under my one moon, which is mine & everyone's,
like life, or love—crazed again—
once more—stupefied as a matter of fact,
without negotiable resources or plans,
discommoded and jittery—how I run on—
moon like a fumbled button, doorknob
on a portal I throw myself against—or did—
who would believe me—she wouldn't—
one more time.

DREAMS

I wake early from a dream of French poetry,
from the wellsprings of it, all rural in the dream:
a cripple in blue britches limps to a mossy well
contradicting himself as he comes.

Morning is a continuation of the dream
—the rusty, crippled hours, trees as if dipped in light syrup,
skaters coasting by, one man in black, drifting with arms folded . . .

I read over a few poems, make some changes in my mind,
dilute fabrications, push across a desert colored red
by sunset, bridge a gap in
the last scene between lovers
now too frail and bored to go on.

My mother was in my dream,
commenting on my looks and the way I dress.
You're too formal, she says.

        the early morning hours
extend generously into day

I read Italian poets; leftwing, outraged poets
from the Sixties (poets who are always leaving home),
and Pasolini,
distorted and enraged by lust,
a concentrate,
a man in a silver sidecar, the late poems
unburdening themselves of poetry

. . . and read a story
about a woman dreaming, who opens

fruit after fruit, orange pulp
and red squashed material
she doesn't understand, who watches her son
place speckled cowries on her sleeping body, a retarded boy . . .

       each dream without relation to the day
catching its breath up ahead,

day a novelty
appearing at the exits of sleep,
a concession stand employee
who is actually your father.

My father once
in a cowboy suit outside school
performing poorly executed rope tricks.

TWO POETS

Do you want children? one of us asked,
but the other, deep in poetry, didn't answer.
We smelled of junk
and wrote of this, and left inked passages
to rest awhile on the tabletop, scratched
into the Formica. *Heroin,* you said,
feeling that poetry glow,
heroin's like the globe, world globe I mean—
set on fire? and stalled out.
The world was our companion volume, the extra,
disinterested party, drunk projectionist,
fronted by the slim boy you ran your fingers over
when he came to collect for something
we could never remember, and ran away.
We thought the cattle were dying
and called the vet
who drove out in his infirmary truck to take a look.
He told us not to get him out there again
unless one of them was actually on the ground.
We watched him leading his ball of dust
back toward town, and some small
and imperturbable sadness arose in us,
some ineradicable softly appealing despair
nothing but a drug could put to rest, and then
one of us got off the beginning of a line,
a few compendious words, before the other cranked the works;
this was us, this was the poetry life.

THE SUBMERGED FIELDS

It's late and someone's almost forgotten
how to write, how to
turn the jubilated rough fields into fields where
the moon scatters pleasantries, fields the wind picks at
looking for bones, fields his ancestors rode over,
died in, where his father's buried
and the misshapen crepe myrtle
sags in sunlight, sags in rain . . .

someone sent out a cover story for his life,
but you know that, you can tell . . .

it's late and someone's almost forgotten
how to convince you he's telling the truth,
how the breeze stirs memories in him,
how the river's an adept of paradise
and each cone and disinterred patch of light
each meadowlark and vole are precious
to someone . . . someone no one talks to anymore
is on the road, it's late
and he's almost forgotten how to speak,
how to convince himself there's enough to go on,
how the fields, rained-on and the crops drowned,
might be married to something else
besides failure, someone who stops
to observe how the light pours through the rain
and the road's washed through to the clay
underlayment which is white and shines,

who gets up late and writes

How beautiful the days are here
and the river matted with ferns touches my heart.

VISITATION

Fall binds itself, sticks itself loosely in tufts
      and fragments into trees, goes bad in an oak,
drains color down the long sleeve of a catalpa
      like a cut getting worse.
The woman who washes at the water fountain is gone now,
      drifting among the avenues;
her place in the plan is kept for her by certain
      small arrangements made years ago and honored in
relays: same bottles, different men. Now the cross-hatched,
      sugary light smells of the open doors of Chinese restaurants;
a breeze sweeps into the slim upper branches of a maple,
      stirs the leaves to a frenzy, fades, and reappears
twirling on the sidewalk; for a second
      there's no pattern to things, no scheme.
The aged couple feeding pigeons by hand, a vicious pair,
      pause; the old man stares straight ahead,
the woman too, adjusting her clothes;
      whatever they see—a moment ago wasn't there.

Fellow passes my bench, wheels his bike
around, screams, leaps off and throws himself lengthwise
onto grass, stares straight into the sun. Odor of alcohol,
this about the only thing these days
produces such floppy flamboyance,
the idea's to give life meaning, drama, I am somebody
kind of buffing, but it always fails. I read Mallarmé,
don't pay attention, try some Baraka,
"The New World" one of the best poems in the new world,
wonder again about B's use of parentheses, what's up
with that, let my attention rise into the sycamores,
dusty crumpled leaves color of shredded cigarettes,
sunlight on the bum again, time when
our good fortune to be alive is treacly with sadness,
but good, affordable feeling, a statutory melancholy,
fine to feel set against the true horrors of our time,
faintly celebratory, sought after by poets
and others of the feeling professions, it gets to you,
but no noticeable difference in passersby, they push
on, it's warm today, day if there was a pond around
there'd be gold dust on the surface, leaves floating
gently nipped by trout. I think of Emily Dickinson's
great poems about the seasons, and lately, so I recall,
I've been thinking of Sir Philip Sidney, of Wyatt
and of the Earl of Surrey who wrote Wyatt's elegy, a formal
and regular practice in those days—Mallarmé continued this—
poets setting themselves at the head of the grave
to bless and keep a foot on the fallen great.
In the anthology not many major practitioners these days,
lonely profession even if a feature of courtly life,
the great always lonely as Socrates taught us, all
of us lonely as the rest of us taught us . . . a friend

I called was weeping, couldn't stop, loneliness again,
if it goes on too long unchecked we make bitter mistakes
or sometimes knock on the neighbor's door and new life begins,
that is, love starts, finds a way
to notice the light in the oaks, soft flight
of words or birds winging over us, the beauty
of mercy, the drunk's delicate fingers,
a figure that connects and exemplifies us. A poem
does this, or the truth admitted. For better or worse,
we admit only universal truths, but there are as many
of the individual variety perhaps, not grave but lasting,
we find these out by living. A breeze snakes along the grass.
It seems to follow sunlight, sunk there.
Now the whole park's in shadow. Sun's still strong
against the upper parts of the eastern buildings, shines
all the way through the top floors of one, exposing
desks, a Brazilian flag, two women gesturing furiously.
Snappy, birdlike, fluttery light; then night suddenly comes.

BONTEMPS

Figure you could spend a thousand years
studying one speck of butterfly dust, then go on
to the next and then ten thousand on the water drop the speck
floats in, the ground-up regurgitated
mucilage its accompanying amoeba has just ejected from its excretal sac
taking up another three thousand years of patient
intent scrutiny, and then the germ in the amoeba's innards
another five hundred years, and the refraction of light passing through this,
the fourth wave or conniption of particles from
the right set of rainbowlike protuberances, take this
as your area of expertise, spend ten millenniums
tracing it back to the source which of course is a sumptuous
spangolem in itself and includes the spurt of burning gasses just now passing
Jupiter's third moon, one faint wisp of this containing
enough hydrogen to power earth for a million years,
take a grain of this and stand by yourself on Copernicus,
in a dusty hole, scrutinize the periodicity of the four hundredth
atom to the left of the Seal of St. John, and wait
your turn with the five billion others who have
themselves spent eternity doing exactly the same
thing, at a slightly different pace,
to explain this, and while you are waiting
under the one trillion billion stars upon which
the molecules—worlds aspin—all quake, each with its own separate
and sonorous rhythm, each awaiting its turn at the mike,
each impatient, put upon, outraged, desperate
like a man in a dark stairwell fighting off thieves,
and while you are waiting think how one
moment of time is enough in which to understand everything,
one glance at a single tree holding up the rain-shattered light, enough,
and then turn back and start over because you remember a miscalculation

somewhere in the third era to the left of the beginning,
and do this several times, all the time maintaining
your place in line, and then you realize it's been going on like this
for years, like somebody's idea of the good life,
or the way each night the cooks and the busboys gather
on DeLawter's back steps and smoke and tell stories
passing a bottle around, eating crab legs, and summer never ends.

HALF-DONE WORLD

I propose to put things differently,
but then I forget to & get lost watching fall decorate the peach trees
& barely know myself. Light fades among the mown yellow grasses.
In Maine the ocean wears a black tuxedo.
Sunlight comes to mind, a return to quiet afternoons, someone
lazing in tall grass. I keep bringing the old love back to mind.
She's gone away for good, but I can't get over it.
I record my voice saying her name, then mimic her
saying I love you. It gets no better,
trails away
into undistinguished pleading and lies. The day
strains against itself, gives up, slides into twilight & soft ex-summer airs.
I'm not trying to tell a story.
I watch my best friend paint, watch him lean into the small square
he's set against an easel dabbing yellow into the field.
More often than not the old men don't pass the old ways on.
The young men walk down the road singing stupid songs
& making promises they'll never keep, & this is familiar.
Love watches itself go to pieces in someone's backyard,
& later we admit we have no explanation for how things turned out.
My friend, with a brush tipped lightly against the canvas,
holds down a world—as dark comes—half-done world, already passed.

LATE RETURN TO MIAMI

So many things provide a ministry.
Oven birds for example, shade, the red hibiscus flowers
above the head of an old man asleep in Miami.
I turned all the way around and
went back the way I'd come; nothing had changed.
It's always like that, someone says, always the same,
only the way we look at it varies. The world, she says,
confirming this, might be one thing only,
a permanent drive-in we circle like teenagers
in flashy cars. It's the aspects confuse us, she says,
almost whatever you want to call it, she says.

A crippled woman
goes mournfully on about her dead son, but
she can't help it. We try to forgive, but
even this is mostly grace. I drink some coffee.
It's pleasant to picture poincianas, locusts in bloom.
At noon, again at two-thirty, the
buttons on an old man's tunic shine; he hasn't moved,
or he's moved and returned.
The beautiful women sip lavender drinks.

I can't get certain beaches out of my head,
folds and configurations, a breeze revising something in the sea oats.
So many draw sustenance from their children.
It's hard to continue, we pass things around,
repeat gestures and look for a way to help.
Every well-marked path
doesn't lead somewhere. Whatever's essential
you find someone making do without it.
Old women talking to themselves remind me of my mother;
such correspondences strike to the bone.

I turn to rivers, poems, the sun-soaked stretch
of sand beyond Fifth Street, go
up the steps, there's a wooden tower you can climb.
Up high, boys tease their girlfriends. They too stumble
around, they too return late, empty-handed.

HISTORY

Behind big windows, on a street of new houses,
women watch egrets settle on lawns, blackbirds
drop from tulip poplars onto the grass.
They're watching the world—one behind each window—
come up with something more subtle
than before. In the garages, naked engines gleam on racks:
blue royal gray like beef when the final membrane
is reached, the rubbery shroud the butcher pulls off
with the hide. The street gleams from rain.
The women know how men make excuses for themselves,
they've heard the excuses. But they are watching
the world distribute it's notice of
revision and reapplication, the leaves upon
which is written on the back of each a tiny cry,
irrepressible now, calling for help.
Help me, the men cry in their sleep,
but the women are standing at the windows
watching the rain slant into the lawn.
They know this is history returning for its wounded.
They will never walk outside to speak
to whatever is weeping out there, if something is,
some force or design in the form of a stranger
down on his knees. Leaves collect in the birdbaths.
It was always worse than they thought,
but they aren't really thinking about it anymore.

SANTA MONICA

Someone was writing this incredibly personal poem
and I was reading it over his shoulder
Santa Monica was in the poem
but you could hardly tell
and the devastating loss of integrity
his wife ranting
his cowardice—these were in the poem
and he was sweating as he wrote it
and looking around as if for spies
I am amazed he didn't see me
but sometimes they look right through you
he went on writing his act of contrition
and memory
expressing his extreme embarrassment and sorrow
at how he selfishly used loved ones
lost the money and the house
sat in the car out in the driveway the last morning
and couldn't think where to go
until someone, a cop maybe, suggested
he go get something to eat, and then after that he drove
to Kansas. There was a weeping blue cypress in the poem
and at one point he was very accurate about how it feels
when on the street the beloved turns you away.
Sometimes, he wrote, *I stand unnoticed at a counter, waiting.*
At last the woman looks at me and asks what.
It was a struggle, for both of us, to get to the next part.

THE WATERS OF THE DEEP

We were trying to keep it conversational,
close to the text,
but I was very nervous that year, all year,
and kept breaking in to express an inexpressible sorrow,
and when we turned around—we
were in the garden—I saw his wife pouring some red liquid into a pot,
red like neon . . . or no,
red like the heroin/blood mix
swirling like the waters of the deep
in a syringe,
and I thought how the narrative, the story
simply branches off in unrecoverable directions,
things mount up, experiences,
the way she said *sulty* for *salty*,
distinguished moments I mean anguished moments,
until sometimes I think I am back in prison,
some medium security place
where I'd look through the fence at cars
turning in to the strip mall,
and as ugly as the mall was with its stores the color of pigeon feathers
and the dust on the cars,
the boarded-up seafood restaurant & the crystal shop,
I'd wish I could go there,
at least use the pay phone in private, call my past up,
maybe my old camp counselor,
tell him I'd be late for dining hall,
but I was on my way.

You can see how it would be possible
simply to go on like this, constructing little scenarios,
foolish responses to life,
to stimuli,

to love and its evasions,
go on tormenting myself
with the vastness of losing propositions,
to say, Well, I'm not sure,
but I think this came after that,
or was it at the same time,
waiting, as if at a bus stop in Puebla,
for someone simply
to describe something in English,
pull a pig's knuckle
from his pocket and pass this around
while he talks in a low voice of a woman
who used to beat him with switches,
something like this,
some way of putting things that captures
something otherwise unendurable,
some last chance exemplified, rain pitting the ditch water
while she sang softly to herself a song
I no longer remember, her voice fading into the rain
and into her life's slow insistence on leaving me.

"It's almost like this," he said, my friend,
lowering his voice,
"yet only collaterally, since what you are saying
ocurred in *your* life, not mine,
but I do think this is what happens generally,
something profound occurs one afternoon in the kitchen
or in the alley where your uncle
broke down and wept,
and later you stand around talking,
hesitating to explain,
to say why, that year you complied

with everything, you kept losing the car keys,
and called your ex-mother-in-law repeatedly
until she took out an order of protection
against you, and then—
what was it?—you had to give up the drugs,
and later—tonight maybe—
after too many cups of coffee,
we stand out back watching a train rattle by,
and when the guy next to you asks
what you are thinking, you say,
'I was thinking of throwing myself under the wheels,'
but that's not it. Right? That's not even close."

EAST END

Framed hard against daylight, against day, plush gray sky slanted west,
we rise, fall down the dune and run at the sea. It's almost calm, snaky under silk,
an army transferring materiel under cover, approaching us. Light picks up
the failed sheen of soaked sand draining. Rock sand, rocks, scoria rubbed
to egg shapes, mottled or striped, some gray, formal, black-suited
dolmen to place on top of a wall you walk by to a funeral—sea rocks.
Up ahead, ponderous clay cliffs, ocher cliffs, broken off, chewed at,
crumbling, stare out to sea. Arches undercut verticals. Each element's
in for the long haul, nothing going anywhere, it's clear; everything repeats itself,
picks up what passes by & uses this, keeps at it. Torn skate purses, crumbled lace of bone,
crab claws, crab shells like tiny tricorns: something awful's happened
under the sea. The dunes rear back, appalled, tumble down and bury themselves
under grass. Something's buried there, that's what it looks like: summer and its dead,
the age sinking deeper. We're following the slink of tideline, watching it run optimistically up
and recede. It goes on rustling, rolling up, the paunchy surf bullying it behind,
orbiculate, unable to repeat itself exactly, unable to conclude, which is the lure.
Sure. One minute to the next nothing's the same, inconclusive, only the invariable
materials, procedure, repetition, the loading docks in continuous operation,
big payloaders, stinking of the Mesozoic, chuffing up, crunching against the ramps,
the enterprise going on under lamplight, firelight and sunny day,
combining or sorting out, slipping one thing inside the frame of another,
using what it has, making do, the same ingredients, same elements
always in short supply, the effort hampered by bad weather
and the torpor agitation replaces, by inexactitude and irrepressible revision,
someone dying on his feet, the light beginning to fail, everything
piled against the same limitation, the transaction now surely giving way
like an ocean turning ponderously on its heel, catching itself in the face
with a blow—a wave, salt-streaked, white-streaked—collapsing and rising again.

AT THIS HOUR

The city deharmonizes in some areas, arms us with breastworks,
yet continues to provide juxtapositions both instructive and beautiful,
a constabulary in the mind,
archways through which light tosses lightly its yellow exigencies,
in others
a sense of the casual ribaldry of existence,
or diverts us down increasingly narrow passageways
until we find ourselves once more leaning out over darkness itself,
unable to confide in our dearest friends, disestablished and bereft,
commonplace characters who have become withdrawn.

The city does this
or the willingness to go . . . to get on with things
does. Without waiting for amplitude to swell in the lower keys
we maintain swampy
and undistinguished unions with desperate characters
to sustain this. It's always best to
hope for the next generation's success, but not so easy.
We don't really care, subdue what we can now, devalue the rest.

A fortune, someone says commenting on this,
would complete things nicely, though today, as the wind picks up,
I am thinking of summer's references, the Rubens exhibit
we got sick in, and then a brief shower of rain,
the city's version of beneficence, falls prostrate
among the tuned up and sparkling late afternoon sunlight,
and the vertigo begins to pass, which is the key, things move along,
the humiliating set of circumstances reverts to type,
and our carefully pleaded argument, love's lost soldier, fades
along the surface rhythms of some obscure chant
playing softly on a junkie's turned-down radio, someone almost peaceful at this hour.